VOICES IN MY HEAD

For Chris, but for whom ....

First published in Great Britain by Black Apollo Press, 2007

Copyright © Terence Moore 2007

A CIP catalogue record of this book is available at the British Library.
ISBN: 9781 906448 004

Voices in my HEAD

by

TERENCE MOORE

BLACK
APOLLO
PRESS

CONTENTS

THE WINDS OF CHANCE AND TIME

Love's darkest truth

Love's darkest truth our poets seldom rhyme.
Love's changeful, treacherous, insecure,
Blown by the winds of Chance and Time,
Contingent, dependent, doubtful, unsure.
What Chance and sweet winds bring together,
Chance and rough gales will pull apart.
Love seldom navigates the foulest weather,
Once striking rocks unmarked on any chart.
If Chance by chance love does not undermine,
Time, evergreen, waits ready in the wings
To step on stage and make of love a mime.
Together Chance and Time pull love's strings.

   I would believe love were not ruled by ifs,
   Yet my life, love's darkest truth admits.

Footprints on the beach

'No man is an island', Donne said.
'Each mind is an island', I claim.
Mine still but barely read,
Blurred prints on the beach – arcane.
Away from the littoral, the interior's more mystery,
A twisted jungle, hard to penetrate.
How I grew from child to man's a history
I cannot trace, only blindly re-create.
No cartographer, X crudely marks the spot
Where mother left, where father died,
Where lovers came and went in lots,
Small clearings in the jungle of my mind.
      If my mind's unknown to me is true,
      How far must I be from ever knowing you?

Is there no help?

The shoulders sag,
The head droops,
The feet drag.
> Is there no help?

The hand shakes,
The wine spills,
The glass breaks.
> Is there no help?

Joints stiffen,
Nerves slacken,
Muscles weaken.
> Is there no help?

Memory falls away,
Words are lost,
Senses all decay.
> Is there no help?

'Take one of this, take two of that',
The siren voices sweetly call,
'Ageing we will forestall.'
> There is some help?

No need for the mind to be ill,
Prozac will lighten despair,
Hope locked in a pink pill.
> There is some help?

Blue pills can ignite a flame
In ageing men grown limp.
Take one to erect the shame
    There is some help?

No help none,
Ageing its course must run,
No help none.
    There is no help.

Ageing's worse than death.
A process we endure.
Death has no cure.
    There is no help,

Except for those blessed by love.
They alone ageing resist.
Love conquers all, they insist.
    There is some help.

A life unled

If only the words I've said
Could be unsaid – if only I'd
Listened, looked and read
The silent pain your eyes did hide.
If only, if only you had stayed,
I might've left my life inside,
Turned to how you, not me, was made,
Learnt to feel why you so often cried.
'If only' tells of a life unled.
Imprisoned by fear, I, by shutting in,
Shut out those chained lives I dread.
If only fear were not my sin.
        'If only's where myself I hide,
        'If only's where all hope's died.

An untenable dualism

No longer will I celebrate the cerebral.
Reason's reigned supreme far too long.
The Enlightenment's unenlightened all,
The mind alone is not to be my song.
Yet never will I denigrate the cerebral.
The mind, no longer ruling by its choice,
Remains a valued province, if now in thrall
To a united state, listening to the body's voice.
The body knows things the mind forgets,
Its voice no choice but a silent cry of pain,
Aching to remind us never to let
Its just demands be ignored again.
> The body's pain should the mind alert.
> Heed its voice, or risk pain's hurt.

The sleep of reason

When reason sleeps the heart awakes
Furtively, first fearful reason only naps,
Catnaps, anxious lest a feeling overtakes
Its bosom mate, logic, boa-like, wraps
Feelings tight, constricting till all feeling's dead.
Its major premise: All feelings misinform.
Its minor premise: Love's a feeling all unread.
Its conclusion: Love must us misinform.
Still reason sleeps; the heart tiptoes free,
Quietly, on pulsing wings, it begins
Dancing to a music only love can hear and see,
Living its heartfelt life, free from reason's sins.
    Reason stirs, stretches, yawns, awakes.
    The poor heart, feigning death, almost breaks.

Experiments in immortality

It sits there,
In a small glass dish,
On my bedside table,
Pink, quiet, obtruding,
Waiting.

Challenging a memento mori –
Calling in the death's head,
Offering a memento vitae,
An amazing offer of an unending,
Vigorous, full-blooded life
To come.

To take or not to take,
That is the question.

To be young again,
To run, to leap, to climb
The highest fells,
Surmount the Munros
One by one.

To hold you in my arms again,
To be at peace with you again,
To watch you all -
Sons and daughter,
Grand-Sons, grand-Daughters,
Grow up, become yourselves,
Grow old and . . .

There the big fat fly waits –

Quick, grind the pill's pink face
To dust and ashes,
Blow it to the four corners.

I *will* die.
I hereby swear
I'll never risk
Immortality.

HOW COULD YOU BE SO BOLD?

Love's alchemy

To transmute lead into gold
Those ancient alchemists dreamed.
How could you be so bold?

My base nature you I told
Was leaden – to you it seemed
Lead could be transmuted into gold.

Could a powerful love so enfold
The fears that in me seethed?
How could you be so bold?

A heart dying, dead and cold,
Your transmuting love redeemed.
Lead at last transmuting into gold?

Your alchemy made a heart grown old
Awaken to a life it'd never dreamed.
How could you be so bold?

Without love's alchemy I'd 've sold
My soul for a sensual dream.
You transmuted lead into gold.
How could you be so bold?

Owing

How much do I owe you? I ask each day,
How can I ever truly reckon the cost?
Golden pounds, silver pence never can repay
Your saving a failing life, so close to lost.
I, like her, was drowning, not waving
Until you dived into a mere of mess.
Lifting my head, you set about saving
Me from my self-enforced duress.
Whenever, running scared, I sought to hide,
Frightened by the bonds now me enlacing,
From dread of losing my own self I often lied.
Yet you stayed until loving I began embracing.

    What I owe I never can repay,
    Except by loving you in every way.

Living

Urinate, defecate, copulate,
Recognise, realise, empathise,
    Add the sum of all those words,
    Life is lived among these verbs.

Understand, undermine, underscore,
Construct, destruct, instruct,
    Add the sum of all those words,
    Life is lived among these verbs.

Impel, propel, compel, expel,
Drive in, drive on, drive out.
    Add the sum of all those words,
    Life is lived among these verbs.

Relish, embellish, cherish,
Care, dare, be aware,
    Add the sum of all those words,
    Life is lived among these verbs.

Inspect, expect, respect,
Fail, prevail, curtail,
    Add the sum of all those words,
    Life is lived among these verbs.

Write, re-write, write again,
Draft, craft to find the form.
        Add the sum of all those words,
        Life is lived among these verbs.

Love, re-love, love again,
Break hearts to mend a heart,
        Add the sum of all those words,
        Life is lived among these verbs.

Laugh, smile and sometimes cry,
Make free with these before you die.
        Add the sum of all those words,
        Life is lived among these verbs.

Afterlife

Soon I'll put down this book, now read,
Mulled its final sentence, reached its last word.
Yet a book put down is a book not dead.
Oh no, a book lives on once the self's disturbed,
Sending quickening ripples across the mind,
Crinkling its surface, changing its light,
Challenging the zones of comfort we fight to find,
Forcing us awake before the last goodnight.
My life too soon, like a book, will close its file,
Yet, like a book, a loved life lives on
In others' lives – I'll stay alive while
Those I've loved still recall my song.
    Keep me alive, my love, once I am dead,
    My afterlife's with you – a life I've never led!

Love lives on

All things must die, except for one.
Life must lose its fight with death,
Death's fight with love – it's never won.

After my dying, a miracle will come.
Our love lives on beyond my final breath.
All things must die, except for one.

With you alive our love's not done.
Our love lives on, though half bereft.
Death's fight with love – it's never won.

Cherish the memories that will still run
Around our life, a quickening thread.
All things must die, except for one.

I would not have you play the nun,
For me, act all alive, not dead.
Death's fight with love – it's never won.

For me, go forth, still seek the sun,
Pursue the love you've always bred.
All things must die, except for one,
Death's fight with love – it's never won.

Afraid

I cannot come to you,
I am afraid.
It's not because of what you do.

Why should I feel this fear of you?
I only know it's how I'm made.
I cannot come to you.

To conquer fear, to see it through,
Would show the fault in me is laid.
It's not because of what you do.

The pristine child would have no clue,
No trace of the fear I've displayed.
I cannot come to you.

I've lost that child, so bright and new,
That fearless child, not now my aid.
It's not because of what you do.

If the child is father to the man were true,
I never would've you betrayed.
I cannot come to you,
It's not because of what you do.

Because of you

Outside, the sky overcast and grey,
Inside, a June-bright, glowing day,
    Because of you.

Outside, the city, a fearful place,
Inside, my world, a brave new space,
    Because of you.

Outside, I act a dozen parts,
Inside, I follow my inmost heart,
    Because of you.

Outside, is cut, is thrust,
Inside, is hope, is trust,
    Because of you.

Outside, success must be won,
Inside, fame need never come,
    Because of you.

Outside, I wear the mantle of a man,
Inside, I dress the man I am,
    Because of you.

Outside, is noise before and after,
Inside, is often subtle laughter,
    Because of you.

Outside's where I have to be,
Inside's where I feel most free,
    Because of you.

THE WORLD IS TOO MUCH WITH US

Getting and spending
A sequel to Wordsworth

Wordsworth, you should not be living at this hour.
Your fear's grown ten times worse than you foresaw.
Not only getting and spending do we lay waste our power,
But each day's mail spurs me to waste more and more.
This flier shouts, 'Rewarding you for buying more.'
A double dose of snake oil lures me on
Promising, 'Greater peace of mind.' A shyster's lore,
Say anything to keep them still on song.
If only any piece of it were true.
All, all is lies – lies for the State's good end.
To serve the great god Economy I too
Must sacrifice on its altars, spend, spend, spend.
      To Waitrose, Tesco, Marks, E-Bay,
      I lift two fingers, as I'm swept away.

Tick-a-box

Right or wrong?
        Tick a box.

I can't tick yes,
I can't tick no,
I can't tick either,
Truth won't go.

True or false?
        Tick a box.

I can't tick yes.
I can't tick no,
I can't tick either,
Truth won't go.

Stop this tick, tick, tick-a-box.
Truth's a wily old fox,
Can't be caught in a prison box.

The question's binary,
No answer could fit.
Truth is n-ary,
Learn that or quit!

An unknown GI

'I do my duty,' he said.
'I obey the orders I'm given.'

ORDER

Conditioning 'enemy combatants',
Also known as 'illegal combatants',
For interrogation –
Hood heads with sacks,
Hessian, black, provided.
Adopt stress position,
Strip naked in freezing cell,
Balls – shock,
Dogs – set on,
Shout, bawl, scream, curse,
Confine them solitary,
Desecrate the Koran,
All allowed.

Torture?
'It's not torture,'
My leader says, 'Just
Special methods of interrogation.'

ORDER

'Illegal combatants',
Imprison without due process,
Extend the time as and when,
Charge the innocents –

Those caught digging wells?
Those caught building mosques?
Those caught teaching the young?
Caught – a bounty on their heads –
By false information, grassed,
The hundred innocents thrown in
With the 'guilty'

'It's just justice.'
My leader says.

In a home for breaking minds,
An unknown GI endlessly repeats,
'I did my duty.'
'I obeyed the orders I was given'.

Rest

Wrest, from this restless life, some rest.
Still the ceaseless chatter in the head.
Dare to set out on a curious quest
To find that space where thought is dead
Yet feelings are alive; refresh the dried-up heart,
Savour the sweet taste of uncluttered time,
Relish the quiet touch of enclosing dark,
Cherish the deep sound of a silent mind,
For a time; wrest from rest a slow return,
Pick up life's chaos with a mended mind,
Face restlessness renewed, with fire to burn,
Accept we're mortal, entwined with our kind.
    Best rest at first seems the wrested rest,
    Rest without wresting at last the best.

If only

If only we'd done it,
But we didn't.

If only we could've,
But we couldn't.

If only I'd listened,
But I didn't.

If only you'd stayed,
But you wouldn't.

If only I could face
Things as they are
Now, here, now.
But I can't.
Never could.

If only I could dump
'If only.'

If only.

Conditional perfect

As life races towards the finishing line
One tense preoccupies the faltering mind,
The tense that tells
What might've been,
What should've been,
What would've been,
What could've been,
But never was.

The tense Grammarians call
The Conditional Perfect,
I call
The tense of Lost Dreams.

The tense rebuking our one-time fears,
Chides our lack of courage at the crux.
The tense that tells
The path we might've taken,
But never did.

The tense that tells
I should've done –
What I so hotly wished to do,
But never did.

The tense that tells
If only I'd've rung,
You might've quickly come,
But I never did.

The tense that tells
The man I could've been,
But never was.
The tense that tells,
'Might've,
'Should've,
'Would've,
'Could've,
Are all forever lost
To 'never did'.
To 'never was'.

Her hair

I followed her hair
Everywhere.

Upstairs, downstairs,
Her hair bouncing
On every stair
Without a care.
Inside, outside,
    I followed her hair
    Everywhere

In the sun her hair lit up,
In the shade the lights went out.
Lit up or lit out
Without a doubt
    I followed her hair
    Everywhere.

Rippling her trimmed hair –
Waves breaking gently
On the sand-white
Nape of her neck
    I followed her hair
    Everywhere.

Honey-coloured her hair,
Not brass, not gold, truly fair.
Hard for me to bear.
    I followed her hair
    Everywhere.

Longing to feel,
Not daring to touch.
Was ever hair
Cherished so much?
Shaking her head,
Swinging her hair
She left,
No words said.
    I'd followed her hair
    Everywhere.

Hidden agendas

They met at the appointed time,
In the duly appointed place,
Clutching hidden agendas.

Neither sought what the other thought,
Neither thought what the other sought.
Each guessed at the other's needs,
Each mistook the other's dream.

Neither listened to the other's words,
Neither read between their lines.
Each had hopes, each had fears,
Each knew pain, each dry tears.

Safe-locked within themselves,
Scarred by a fractured past,
Neither dared close the abyss,
Neither dared risk a kiss.

They left at the appointed time,
Heading for a different place.
Still clutching hidden agendas,
Still afraid their truth to face.

WORDS ARE NOT NEEDED
TO BE HEARD

'What I say is meaningless.'
John Lennon

'If only, if only I could find the words'
The lover cries, the lover lies.
Words are not needed to be heard.

The best of words can sound absurd,
Hollow, echoing with a strangled sigh.
If only, if only I could find the words

Is the wrong cry. To be heard
Passion must push words aside,
Words are not needed to be heard.

Toss 'love' in the air, love for you reserved?
Suppose love no longer here resides,
Then if only, if only I could find the words

Is false, words for dead love are undeserved.
The true lament is for the love that died.
Words are not needed to be heard.

To remain silent then, unheard
Until our words with true feelings tied.
'If only, if only I could find the words'
Words are not needed to be heard.

'The intolerable wrestle'
T.S.Eliot, East Coker

I cannot put my thoughts in prison,
They wander in a desert like bedouins roaming,
Beyond the power of any phrase to christen.

Or truly are my thoughts the ones in prison?
My words occasional visitors, departing
To leave my thoughts still unchristened.

Or truly are my feelings the ones in prison?
Disallowing any words to visit, feelings
Beyond the power of any phrase to christen.

Or truly are my meanings the ones in prison?
Finding no words apt for their releasing.
Will I ever see my meanings christened?

Thoughts, feelings, meanings all in prison.
Awaiting a wordsmith for their unlocking.
Myself I cannot escape myself's own prison.

Only in dreams do I walk free from prison,
Thoughts, feelings, meanings dancing – not
Beyond the power of any phrase to christen,
Joy-filled, dreaming, telling the world my lot.

Yourselves

I prefer plurals to singulars.
The singular is so absolute.

Do I love you, your very self?
Not knowingly.
I love you+s, yourselves,
Yes, truly.

I love the ways
You insist on being fair,
Both plates have exactly
The same number,
Three beetroots each,
Two biscuits, turned in.

I love the ways
You descend the stairs
Like Venus from the foam,
Dressed in a dream.

I love the ways you
Search for whom you are.
Iyengar, hatha, kundalini,
Ways to explore the selves you are.

I love the ways you fall upon
Free singing, free dancing,
Freeing you from the head,
Releasing the crumpled heart.

I love the ways you
Care for me
At all times, rich and poor.
Is that what they call amour?

Rhyming

Glove,
Heavens above!
Throw in 'dove'
All rhymes
For 'Love'.

Unless, like the Great One,
You cheat!

Allow eye-rhymes,
'Move' and 'prove'
To rhyme with 'love,
Or, say, 'loove.'

Or morph 'move' and 'prove'
Into 'muve' and 'pruve'.

Then
I must my love
Pruve,
Or else
Muve on!

Revising – Nero's – springtime

The scene – the street café – upstairs.
Files, folders, papers, books and notes
Strewn on tables among abandoned coats,
The Young, revising, singly or in pairs.

Revising to enter the last exam saloon,
Sipping their skinny lattes,
Smoke curling from their coffin nails,
Preparing as the final Tripos looms.

To revise is to prepare, to what end?
For some the thirst's for a first,
For others the word's a third,
For all the degree's the key
Unlocking the gate to a secret fate.

Should I, an aged, watching man, take note?
My final too is close at hand.
No one gains a first in Tripos Death,
Passing's assured, honoured or honourless.
Once passed, the future's blind.

What shall I tell them
As they revise?
Say nothing, old man,
In their young eyes
You have nothing to tell!

Love's pronouns

I am you,
You are me,
They are them,
We are us.

Each is the other,
Both are one.
Myself is yourself,
Yourself is myself.

Two into one will go,
As any bed must know.

Strong the coupling,
Tender the parting.
Sweet the rejoining,
Gentle the leaving.

Riddle-me-ree,
I still am free,
Free not to be free.
Riddle-me-ree,
You too are free,
Free not to be free.

I am you,
You are me.
They are them,
We are us.

On the necessity of pain

What in life we need, alas, is pain.
Yet always pain we try to burke.
Without pain, alas, we could not life sustain.

Pain's our sharp signal to maintain
Defences against the many ills at work.
What in life we need, alas, is pain.

Memories of past hurt retained,
To present dangers us alert.
Without pain, alas, we could not life sustain.

Pain tells us not to take that route again,
The route that brought the deepest hurt.
What in life we need, alas, is pain.

The hurt with the longest, deepest reign
Lies buried in love's loss from words unheard.
Without pain, alas, we could not life sustain.

Ignore those who would pain restrain.
Pain's a signal to cherish for its worth.
What in life we need, alas, is pain.
Without pain, alas, we could not life sustain.

EACH MAN IS AN ISLAND

Each man is an island

'No man is an island', Donne wrote.
My life's tried to prove him wrong.
In childhood I learnt to burn every boat,
Alone on my island I was strong.
Warily each dawn I'd patrol my beaches,
The night could bring landings to repel.
Some fought like Vikings off leashes,
Others were a deal easier to expel.
Child once – old, I'm building a quay,
Next I must try lighting a fire.
Each boat sails past indifferently,
None turns to the bent man building his pyre.
     No man an island true.
     Each man an island too.

Be yourself!

Consider this day.
Already I have been:
Sincere and devious,
Clever and stupid,
Vivid and insipid,
Generous and mean,
Lively and dull,
Truthful and spinful,
And points between –
So what am I?

Devious and sincere?
Stupid and clever?
Insipid and vivid?
Mean and generous?
Dull and lively?
Spinful and truthful?
And points between.

Consider this day.
Already I've acted:
Father and child,
Lover and loather,
Sage and clown,
Teacher and taught,
Mate and loner,
Creator and destroyer,
Truther and liar,
And points between –
So who am I?

Child and father?
Loather and lover?
Clown and sage?
Taught and teacher?
Loner and mate?
Destroyer and creator?
Liar and truther?
And points between.

Young once, I the questioner,
Addressing the imperative
Strode the Fells,
Climbed the peaks,
Lay among the sheep,
Begged the clouds to part,
Willing a voice,
Firm, fatherly,
In basso profundo,
To answer.

The clouds never parted,
No profundo voice ever spoke.

Forsaken, I learnt to endure
The silence.
Slowly, slowly a light dawned:
Disobey the imperative!

Hunting my one and only,
My true, my unique self,
Hunted a wily will o' the wisp –
My single self's not extant
Uttered by an idiot,
'Be yourself!' is an imperative
To beat the unbeatable

So in age what remains?
Only of my teeming selves
To be aware.

Going deaf

As I nudge up to Death,
Or truer, as Death approaches me,
I find I gradually grow deaf.

Not simply deaf to people's breath,
But deaf to people's agony.
As I nudge up to Death.

No longer can I exhort myself
To listen to others confidingly.
I find I gradually grow deaf.

A slow retreat into an inner self.
No violent raging, just quiet ageing
As I nudge up to Death.

Is my place now on the shelf?
Or in a don's den, retiring dutifully?
I find I gradually grow deaf.

We deaf can hear ourselves
Whilst others we're ignoring mutely,
As I nudge up to Death,
I find I gradually grow deaf.

Waning memory

To enter a room
To fetch a thing,
    And know not what.

To need a name
To tell a friend,
    And know not who.

To want a word
To solve a puzzle,
    And know not which.

To take a tool
To fix the fuse,
    Forgetting how.

Not to remember,
And know not why,
That's the stage before you die.

Unilateral love

For me she doesn't care –
A cheery, careless wave –
Only for her I truly care.

When next we part I swear
Not to care, to be brave.
For me she doesn't care.

When we're apart I wear
My brave, insouciant gaze.
Only for her I truly care.

When we're together I bear
No trace of the lonely days.
For me she doesn't care.

When she never rings I tear
Her apart in a million ways.
Only for her I truly care.

Take me away – somewhere, anywhere,
To bedlam where mad lovers rave.
For me she'll never truly care,
That I'll never learn to bear.

Sensible love

Sensible love I never knew I craved.
'Can love be sensible?' you said.
Not when love's young, perhaps when aged.

Young love cannot but be crazed,
Hot, heedless, for love all else is fled.
Sensible love I never knew I craved.

The bond between us didn't fade,
Shaped by way of the life we led.
Not when love's young, perhaps when aged.

Sensible love's late role we've played
Once tense love's time is dead.
Sensible love I never knew I craved.

Now trusting, laughing, little at all depraved,
Two minds as well can meet in bed.
Not when love's young, perhaps when aged.

'In tempore oportuno', said the ageing sage,
Respect love's seasons, enjoy what each us fed.
Sensible love I never knew I craved.
Not when love's young, perhaps when aged.

Myselves

I prefer plurals to singulars.
The singular is so absolute.

To the cry,
'Who am I'?
The silence is deafening.
To the cry,
'How many are you?'
The silence is lessening.

I am the one who listens,
I am the one who listens and may care,
I am the one who tries to see
Into the dark forest of another's soul.

I am the one hanging on – just
The grip on the rock is definitely
Weakening, I'm suspended
Over a drop into infinity.

I am the one crouched behind the coats
In the corner of the dark cupboard,
Fearing someone will notice
I'm no longer around.

Which is me?
I do not know.
I only know
I need to be more me
To be closer to you.

AS IF THERE WERE NO TOMORROW

Carpe diem

'As if there were no tomorrow'
Tells a story – time's not on our side.
Come the day there is no tomorrow.

When no hours are left us to borrow,
When our life has almost died,
No longer 'as if'. There is no tomorrow.

Will our story be naught but sorrow,
Mourning all the days we've let slide,
Come the day there is no tomorrow?

Let's resolve our love does follow
The rhythm that runs with time's tide.
As if there were no tomorrow.

The present perfect, no present hollow,
Still refusing to let our love hide,
Come the day there is no tomorrow.

Only now have we time to borrow
A space for our spirits to ride.
'As if there were no tomorrow',
Come the day there is no tomorrow.

Age

'The Body goes to the making of Man'
John Locke

Age, my love, is a state of mind
They say – those who say do not know
My body – what flesh knows is unkind,
Memory's failing, clumsy acting grows,
Wine is spilt, dear friends are mislaid,
The heartbeat quickens, the stairs grow steep
Love's long-standing debts still unpaid,
Nights fragmented, only broken hours of sleep.
It's the body, not the mind, that rules.
'Not so', says Mind, 'Yes so', says Body.
Resolve the dispute, love, which are fools?
Neither at the last – both need each other fitfully.
    Age, my love, is not a state of mind,
      Unless the body its own truth can find.

A response to Dylan Thomas' incitement to rage.

I will not rage against the dying of the light
Useless to rage – bemoan my coming death.
I shall go quietly into that last goodnight.

When rage is rightly tuned, rage is right.
Rage against times wasted, now bereft.
I will not rage against the dying of the light.

Striking heroic poses, however seeming bright,
Powerless to prolong life's determined debt.
I shall go quietly into that last goodnight.

Best, surely, to accept the hour's come for flight.
To where? To up or down, to each I'm deaf.
I will not rage against the dying of the light.

My flight's to somewhere out of sight.
No everlasting life awaits my final breath.
I shall go quietly into that last goodnight.

You, my love, may recall the dizzy heights
We've reached – each day in life defying death.
I will not rage against the dying of the light,
I shall go quietly into that last goodnight.

A prayer to my body

Dear Body, listen, I depend on you
Absolutely – were you to crumble
Crumple, crease, what would I do?
Hear myself begin to mumble?
What, dear Body's in store for me?
Vascular dementia? Alzheimer's lot?
Please, please, not cerebral atrophy,
At least not yet – not blood-flow blocked.
When brain cells shed like autumn leaves,
It's time to go – to pack it in.
Self no longer self deceives,
Body battling Will will surely win.
    You and me, let's act as one,
    Let's go together, our job's done.

Love's symbiosis

Our love is reckoned a kind of symbiosis.
Is it commensual, mutual or inquiline?
What, my love, is the experts' diagnosis?
Commensual? – only one of us gains over time,
The other, they say, is not 'adversely affected'.
True, I've gained, but surely not me alone.
Mutual? – a term more pointedly directed,
Since, yes, for each of us our love has grown.
Inquiline? – perhaps in those early days
I did live within you – a nutrient host
Most generous till your patience waned,
Ejecting me to stand on my own coast.
     Perhaps, my love, our love is oxymoronic,
     Dependently independent – a new symbiotic!

Our life's an oxymoron
(after you asked how things were)

Our life, my love, is an oxymoron.
We're separate and together,
We're separately together,
We're together separately,
We're together and separate.

Only one because
We are two,
Only two because we are one.

It was not always so.
Before I was one,
Independently one.
Because I was strong?
Because I was afraid.

Independence is strength
Only where dependence is strong.
We can't be one
Without being two.

We are one and two,
Two and one.
Add two and one,
The sum's never three,
Just one, or even two.

I'd have it no other way.
And you?

Clouds

How many moods do the clouds reflect?
Who will assay their subtle shapes and weight?
Only the moody man the clouds inspects
Searching for an icon of his troubled state.
Nimbo-stratus portends heavy rain as I,
More nimbo-cirrus, foresee a frenzied squall,
My bleak mood mirrored in a darkening sky,
On you my louring blame will surely fall.
Cirrus, whose filaments of grey-white hair,
Recall care-free days we laughed and played,
Slips up the heavens, cirro-cumulus is there,
Shutting out the sun, reminding me of darker days.

      Only stratus clouds reflect our subtlest moods,
      Layer upon layer with depths imbued.

Catharsis

Words to purge the past.
Phrases to cleanse by stages.
Poems to scrub the soul.
        Might these bring healing?

Depends how deep you dig.
Pushing through the soft soil,
Striking the hard-faced rock,
        The first steps to the tomb.

The testing time comes later,
When the spinning, biting drill
Hits the vibrant nerve, screaming
        Stop!

Drilling, the pain hurts,
The frightened mind backs off,
The wounded heart hides.
        Pain sounds the retreat.

Can the hurt heart
Stop hiding?
Face its pain
        Find true healing?

Reaching the tomb,
Shining a torch on bleached bones,
Reliving their story, leaving,
        Opens deep healing.

The unlooked-for moment,
The unbidden flash,
The blessed release – a mystery, a gift.
        The skeleton mutating.

HEADS OR TAILS

The toss

Heads he loves me,
Tails he loves me not.
Tails, tails I want it to be.

Heads will force me, sadly,
To engage with love's plot.
Heads he loves me.

Tails will leave me free.
Please, Fate, make tails my lot.
Tails, tails I want it to be.

Heads will forever curb me,
Hold me fast to one spot.
Heads he loves me.

Heads I'm afraid it'll be.
Tails I've never got!
Tails, tails I want it to be.

Heads or tails, what's to see.
Life comes out of a pot.
Heads he loves me.
Tails, tails I want it to be.

Tidal love

No one may tell you so I'll
Tell a sailor's tale.
Love is tidal,
Ebbs and flows,
Never still, never stable.
Diurnal, as the Sun and Moon
Contend.

When the ebbing ebbs
Recall the flowing,
When the flowing flows,
Recall the ebbing.

Hapless, no sailor forgoes a hopeless dream –
A love steady, unchanging, constant
Till the end of Time.
I, one of the sailors.

Hapless, no sailor descries the orbit
Love must run,
Locked forever in its diurnal round.
I, one of the sailors.

Indifferent, hapless, love remains
Tidal.

The lesson

They're at it all the time,
Fuck, fuck, fuck, fuck.
Just my bleeding luck
She's his alone, not mine.

We tried our chat-up tricks.
I expounded Chomsky's grammar.
For her he had no touch of glamour.
Odd – the terms are twins.

He listened while she spoke,
Heard her fears, her needs, her hopes.
Smiled in to her shining eyes,
Comforted her tearful cries.

I talked of fears and hopes,
My fears, my hopes,
Eloquent as I spoke.

They're at it all the time –
Fuck, fuck, fuck, fuck.
Just my bleeding luck
She's his alone – not mine.

I wonder why?

Hide and seek

The sun plays hide and seek with the ponderous clouds,
Nipping behind dark nimbus, slipping behind cirrus,
Whose filaments of grey-white hair less hiding allowed
Than the blazing sun might find within a cumulus.
You, my sun, play hide and seek with me.
Sometimes I feel you burning hot and bright,
You're all I seek – till dark nimbus dims you silently.
Is that nimbus strato-, alto-, cirro-? I cannot tell its height,
Though on each cloud cloudicians confer a degree.
Strato- so low, alto- higher, cirro- highest of all.
How high the nimbus obscuring you from me?
My gravest fear, cirro-nimbus has you in thrall.
     Come out, my sun, your heat will not me melt.
     Custom says the hider should the seeker help.

Spinning

Cobwebs are what spiders spin –
Tensile, intricate, manifold, oblate –
Spun to entrap all blunderers in,
A life to sustain a life, the victim's fate.
Spiders spin to live, we spin to conjure proofs,
To lobby for our lives, phrase-faking just to win.
Spin-laden, our hapless victim's the black fly truth.
No spider ever fakes, nor suffers our original sin.
Truth-telling's a burden human beings bear,
Telling lies lies way beyond a spider's mind,
Truth's uncomfortable, the happiest unaware.
Truth we say we seek, yet often dread to find.
    Side-stepping truth, we're all complicit,
    Spinners all, not caring truth to solicit.

Shagging

To shag or not to shag
That's my question.
Should it be love in our age
That licenses a shag,
I'm ready to whisper the love phrase,
With mental fingers crossed
Behind my moral back.

Shagging is never pure, never simple.
It comes not trailing clouds of glory,
But with fierce, sharp, paradoxical pain,
Being too close, aching to be afar.

Love, they say, redeems the shag,
Renders it holy, pure, divine.
The shag, surprised by chance,
Procreates an alien, unredeemed
Careless love – the rapture unlooked-for,
Without a past, with no future tense,
Only a present perfect.

The male mirage
A touch of reality
Dispels.

MY GODS, MY DEMONS

My gods, my demons

My gods are on the Fells,
On tops of mountains,
In woods, in trees,
In chortling, flashing rivers.

My gods are in my tears
Over the good deeds
Good people enact
Unthinkingly.

My gods are me-made,
Some are jubilant,
All created by me,
Who was created by you.

My demons are me-made too,
Made from the stuff of my life.
Not by you.

The unloved child morphs love
Sour, curdling into hate,
Not only of women
But of preying men.

The demon distrust succoured.
The demon hopeless helped.
The demon failure fostered.
The demon despair tended.

My demons are losing their fight,
My gods have almost won,
Hate morphed back to love,
You and I becoming one.

Tears

I want, I want to cry.
No tears come.
Why, oh why, oh why?

Perhaps because I lie,
Hiding the things I've done.
I want, I want to cry.

Perhaps because I fly
The ghosts I can't outrun.
Why, oh why, oh why?

Can I before I die
Open a heart still dumb?
I want, I want to cry.

The tears you would reply,
Will flow if trust is done.
Why, oh why, oh why?

Look, look these eyes,
Tears you've started to run.
I want, I want to cry.
Why, oh why, oh why?

Self-love

Alone, I'm all at ease with my body's state,
Controlling for myself its slow, rising tension.
Feeling for myself alone what's at stake,
Right timing no longer even a question.
Knowing with deft fingers where and when
And what to touch, to stroke caressingly,
When to pause, when softly to begin again,
Timing the rapture of release blessedly.
Alone, never a need to ever feign delight,
Coupled, a need to soothe the limp, worried other's
'How was it for you this our special night?'
'Wonderful', you lie, acting like their mother.
    Empty, spinning words – I long to be alone,
    Find me good love – maybe I'll atone.

Appearance and reality

The way they show it,
'Love' is easy:
The close embrace,
The long, slow kiss,
The hurried tug
At shirt and skirt,
The convenient fall,
The accommodating bed,
Or couch, as the case may be.

The way it is:
The clumsy hug,
Heads bumping,
Left or right?
Lips awry,
The missed kiss,
Fumbling fingers finding
Buttons unbuttonable,
Fasteners unfastenable,
Stumbling against a chair,
Or couch, as the case may be.

Will we ever want them
To show us
What we all know?

Walls

Hadrian built his wall against marauding Picts
Antonine's strove to fend off savage hordes.
Mine, deeper and stronger than either, mixed
Not dry turf and old stones but steel, mind-forged,
Barbed in tiers, impossible for any Pict to cross.
None ever did till, striding the vallum's crest,
You appeared, alone, unarmed, impervious to loss,
Tougher than any Pict, better than Scotland's best.
Did I run up a white flag? – lose my heart?
Not all at once did my defences begin to tumble,
Not till you turned away, as if from me to part.
Straightway my hard-fought pretences crumbled.

    Walls shut love out, keeping hearts locked in.
    Pierce my wall, my love, unlock the heart within.

Balancing act

The old seesaw I see it still, an ageing brown,
Still, in the playground, come wet, come shine.
In childhood, alone, astride I'd go up or down,
Fleetingly a perfect poise was sometimes mine.
Now in agehood, striving still to find,
My balance, a perfect poise my holy grail,
A still point, my self's at last defined.
Do I just dream a dream, am I so frail,
So helplessly teetering – an ageing seesaw,
Swinging heartwise up, mindwise down,
Never certain who I really am, never truly sure
What to believe, while in words I sadly drown.
    Balancing body and soul, heart and mind
    Is an exercise for gods, not humankind.

STUMBLING ABOUT IN THE DARK

Un-understanding

When, when will the light dawn?
When, when will my eyes open?
When, when will the blind one see?

Stumbling about in the dark,
I knock against your moods,
Carelessly stamp on your heart.

In the dark, feeling for a switch
I'm fingering a cold, bare wall.
Between us a perpetual night,
Me, struggling to find the light.

Help, help me turn on that light,
Help, help me open my eyes,
Help, help the blind one to see.

I hate the dark.

On leaving

'I'll be in touch', you said.
As if we'd ever been
In touch, in or out of bed.

Unheard my words, never read
My silent signals, myself all unseen.
'I'll be in touch', you said.

Heart open wide, yearning to be led
To an 'in touch' matching my dream.
We never were, in or out of bed.

Your 'in touch' fond illusions fed.
I believed 'in touch' might mean,
'I'll be in touch', you said.

Were you by me misled?
Your 'in touch' only ever seemed.
We never were, in or out of bed.

So another coupling's dead.
'In touch' only ever deemed.
'I'll be in touch', you said.
We never were, in or out of bed.

Needing

As the lock needs the key,
As the arrow needs the bow,
As the rose needs the rain,
  So, my love, I need you.

As the kiss needs the other,
As the day needs the night,
As the dark needs the light,
  So, my love, I need you.

As the mind needs the heart,
As the word needs the mind,
  So, my love, I need you.

As the beloved needs the lover,
As the lover needs the beloved,
  So, my love, I need you!

As love needs hate,
As courage needs fear,
  So, my love, I need you.

Hiding from the hurt

Stop, stop hiding from the hurt,
The hurt of the loveless child.
That hurt never was your just desert.

Like a sand-timer, a false thought invert,
Turn upside down the sense you're reviled.
Stop, stop hiding from the hurt.

Face the loneliness, true, undeserved,
The tear-damp pillow, grief too deeply filed.
That hurt never was your just desert.

Discarded, I quietly grew berserk,
Abandoned – from a mother's love exiled.
Stop, stop hiding from the hurt.

Wearing a mask to hide the hurt
Never stopped the heart running wild.
That hurt never was your just desert.

Your taking off the mask let me revert
To a time before my soul was all ways riled.
Stop, stop hiding from the hurt.
That hurt never was your just desert.

Should: a mean modal

Should I not come in
When the door's open wide,
I would always bear
The burden of regret.
Should I not enter in,
Not entering would be my sin.
   'Should', conditional.

I should, if the door's open wide,
Enter in.
I should do what a man must do,
If I knew what real men did.
   'Should', obligation.

I should have entered in
When the door was open wide.
I should have played the Man.
'I should have' always tells
A sad, sad story.
   'Should have', conditional past perfect.

The Conditional Past Perfect points
To chances lost,
To paths not taken,
To a past imperfect;
'Was going to',
   'Never did'.

The state I seek is
Present perfect,
An impossible dream?

Life of the mind

The life of the mind
Is the only life, some say.

They could not be more wrong.
Yet believing their words wise
I ignored my heart's lives.

Exercising iron control,
Capping a seething world,
Surface-wise seemingly composed.

Never for a second allowing
The force within
To become the force without.

Till one day the cap burst,
Erupting corrosive, burning, acid
Hate on all, all cursed.

Only a lover stayed.

Did they know once
The eruption was recapped,
A new – human – being
Just might emerge!

The difference

What does the child have
That Age has lost?
      Fresh eyes.

What has Age got
The child has not?
      Blind sight.

What does the child have
That Age has lost?
      A pristine heart.

What has Age got
The child has not?
      Broken hearts.

What does the child have
That Age has lost?
      Sparkling hopes.

What has Age got
The child has not?
      Shattered dreams.

What does the child want
That Age no longer wants?
      The whole world.

What does the child need
That Age still needs?
      Love unconditioned.

What does the child know
That Age no longer knows?
      A day is forever.

What does the child not know
That Age knows too well?
      Time's a galloper.

What does the child have
That Age has lost?
      Troubles ahead.

What has Age got
The child has not?
      Troubles behind.

What does the child have
That Age has lost?
      A life to live.

What has Age got
The child has not?
      A death to live.

PLAYING WITH HOMOPHONES

Wring/ring

Wringing my heart's hands,
Wringing as I sit waiting,
Waiting for you to ring.
End my wringing by ringing.

Rang/wrang

In the end you never rang,
While grief's hands
My heart wrang dry.

Wrung/rung

The last tear's wrung
The last call's come,
The last bell's rung.
The last sob's done.

No/know

Should, my busied love, you learn
One thing from me,
Learn to say, 'no'.
'No' you most need to know.

Idol/idle

My Idol's never idle,
She's busier than a bee,
Whilst I, her idle Idol,
Fill the role I am to me.

Knight/night

Knights of today are not
Knights of yore.
No distressed maiden,
Sobbing in the night
Can hope her own white knight
Will slay her dragons of the night.

Sword/soared/sawed

I carry my sword
Wherever I go.
Sometimes it's high,
Sometimes it's low.

Never would my sword've soared,
If ever my sword
Should've been sawed
Off.
Oh no!

Feat/feet

Feats can be noble,
Feats can be heroic.
When life hits hard,
Just getting to our feet
Becomes a noble, heroic feat

Weigh/way

Penser est peser.
To think is to weigh,
To juggle, to struggle
To find my way.

Knew/new

If ever I knew
The good in the new,
I would know
To say 'No'
To the bad in the old.

Eye/I

The Eye that sees all,
Itself it cannot see.
Behind the Eye lies
The 'I' that sees the Eye.
Itself it cannot see.
I/Eye, Eye/I

Raised/razed

Remember, however proud you be,
What you've raised
May be erased,
Your life's work razed
Totally.

Urn/earn

Ashes in an urn,
The end our bodies earn.
Our soul not so confined,
Flying beyond mind.
Where it goes,
Nobody knows.

Oral/aural

Between the word spoken
And the word heard
Lies a great rift.
Oral to aural's
A suspect gift.

Gilt/guilt

Family bonds begin
Gilt-edged,
End guilt-edged.

Bridal/bridle

Lift the bridal veil,
A kiss slips the bridle in.

Hole/whole

Down the hole
Lies the whole.
Within the whole
Lies a hole.
Down the hole ...

Wrap/rap

Wrapped tight in a time-hardened shell,
The seeming-safe self's unsafe.
Release the quivering child within,
Rap, my love, rap on my wrapped self.

Alone/a loan

Face it, we're alone,
Life's a short, short loan.
Death, cancelling the loan,
Ends ever being alone.

Tier/tear

Tier upon tier
Tears tier.
Falling in tiers
Tear after tear.

Humerus/humorous

If by chance you knock
Your funny bone,
The humerus isn't humorous
At all.

Plane/plain

Boarding a plane,
It's plain is
A flight from reason!
Boarding our plane
Plainly shows
Reason does not reign.

Miss/amiss

With this Miss
Nothing was amiss
Until she strayed –
A bad Miss!

Prey/pray

Each prey prays each day
Not to be the prey.
Each preyer prays each day
To kill the prey that prays.

Rain/reign/rein

My month fills dykes,
Rain reigns supreme.
Arraign Pisces:
Not reining in the rain.

Scent/sent

Her scent sent
A multitude of men
Crazy.

Write/rite/right

Writers to write
Indulge in rites,
Hoping to create
The right mood
To write.

Printed in the United Kingdom
by Lightning Source UK Ltd.
PP763000001B/1/A